Occupational English Test For Nurses HINTS By Virginia Allum

ISBN 978-1-291-79505-9

Contents

1. What is the OET Writing for Nurses sub-test?

The OET Writing sub-test is a test with a specific focus on nursing and takes 45 minutes. The task is usually to write a letter of referral. The referral may be to a nursing home or a community nurse. Occasionally the letter is to advise or inform a patient or group e.g. a school nurse may send a letter to inform students and parents about a health issue.

Many nurses find this task difficult as it is rare for nurses to write letters of referral any more. These days, discharge letters are written on the computer often following a given template. Copies are sent as referral letters. The writing task is still relevant for nurses, however, as nurses need to be able to select and organise relevant information to write nursing notes, incident reports and variances on clinical pathways.

You will receive the task and stimulus materials so you can prepare your letter of referral. The **task** is found at the end of the stimulus materials. It will ask you to write a letter of referral to a particular person. The **stimulus material** is similar to the patient's discharge information you may be familiar with. The material will include personal and medical background as well as a discharge plan.

The first five minutes of the test is reading time. During this time, you may study the task and notes but may not write, underline or make any notes. You will need to work out very quickly which information is needed for your letter. Whilst much of the information is included in the discharge plan, other information may be scattered throughout the stimulus material.

For the remaining 40 minutes you may write your response to the task. You receive a printed answer booklet in which you must write your response. This also has space for rough work. You may write in pen or pencil.

Make sure you spend a few minutes making a plan of your letter. You need to set out the plan of each paragraph including the points for each paragraph.

What do the marking criteria mean?

Criterion	Description
Task fulfilment	1. Have you followed the instructions of the task? 2. Are you writing the correct type of letter? 3. Is the letter the correct word length?
Use of appropriate language	1. Did you use formal language rather than 'chatty' language which is more appropriate for a letter to a friend? 2. Did you use medical terminology where necessary? **If you are writing to a colleague, you may use some medical language.** 3. Is the tone of the letter non-judgemental? **e.g. 'The patient has difficulties with compliance' is better than 'The patient doesn't try to take his medication at all.'**
Understanding of the stimulus material	1. Did you scan the stimulus material for relevant facts? 2. Did you understand abbreviations and symbols used? e.g. ↑ SOB (increasing shortness of breath) 3. Did you only use relevant facts in your answer? **That is, facts which go under the paragraph headings of your letter. It is quite common for the stimulus material to contain extra material which is not needed for your letter.**
Use of correct grammar and text cohesion	1. Can you make sentences using correct grammar forms? Note that the passive is often used in formal letters. 2. Do your sentences make sense (have cohesion)? 3. Make use of commonly used collocations.
Use of correct spelling and punctuation	1. Do you know how to use commas and full stops? 2. Use of capital letters. 3. Can you spell common terms used in medical English? 4. **Always** spell anything on the stimulus material correctly!

Overall task fulfilment

1. Have you followed the instructions of the task?

You will know what your role is and you will know who you are writing to. For example, you may be a Charge Nurse on a ward writing to a community nurse or a manager of a nursing home. **Understanding the task instructions is one of the most important aspects of the test.**

Initially you may write:

I am writing to refer Mr X to you **for care and support.**

I am writing to refer Mr X to you **for follow-up care.**

I am writing to **transfer** Mr X back to your care. (Mr X was living in a nursing home, went to hospital and is now returning to the nursing home)

I am writing to **transfer** Mr X for rehabilitation.

Remember that you explain the reason for the letter at the beginning but **only as a summary.** The details of what you are requesting will be written in the final paragraph.

2. Are you writing the correct type of letter?

Generally you will be writing a referral letter. It may be to a nursing home or to a community nurse. You may be transferring a patient back to a nursing home or writing a letter to a GP requesting a service.

1. Who are you writing to?

Use the correct salutation and write the address correctly. We will look at this later.

2. What is the reason for writing? Explain the main purpose of your letter at the start, e.g.

- discharge letter for a patient going home and needing nursing support
- transfer letter for a patient going to a nursing home
- discharge letter for a patient going home and needing follow-up care by their GP

Be clear about the level of urgency of your letter e.g.

- 'The patient will need to have an INR in two days' time'.
- 'The patient requires suture removal in a week'.

3. What treatment did the patient receive?

The patient has a surgical history

Think about the sort of information you'll talk about.

Name of the operation

Does the patient have a wound?

Does the patient need sutures /clips / staples removed?

Does the patient need help with their personal hygiene?

The patient has a medical history

Does the patient need help with personal hygiene?

Does the patient need help with mobility?

Does the patient need education or help to use a glucometer or CPAP machine for example?

The patient has a mental health history

Does the patient need encouragement to continue treatment?

Has the patient started a new medication?

4. What is the discharge plan? What new medication has been prescribed or what medication has been restarted? What physio has been started? What equipment has been supplied?

5. What complications did the patient suffer? Were there any abnormal events during the operation or in the post-operative period? What happened?

6. What are the post-op instructions? When will sutures or clips be removed? When does the patient need a dressing change? When does the patient need a blood test?

3. Is the letter the correct word length?

The letter must be 180 – 200 words. **It is very important that you stick to the word limit.** You are going to write around four paragraphs in your letter. Each paragraph will therefore contain around 45-50 words. This means that you will write a topic sentence to start the paragraph and write two or three sentences to support the topic sentence.

Appropriateness of language

Type of language

- Professional letters use a formal style of writing.

- Informal language such as slang, colloquialisms and jargon is often used in informal letters. The only time you may use informal language is if it is clear that you are writing to a well-known colleague.

- Informal SMS texting is never used in formal letters.

As the OET writing test is a test of your ability to form correct sentences using appropriate language, you will need to use formal language. For example, 'keep an eye on' (spoken) is the same as 'monitor' (written)

Organisation of your material

1. Who are you writing to?

Use the correct salutation to begin and end the letter. A 'salutation' is a greeting.

* If the recipient's name and title is given in the task information, you should use them.

* In Australia, you should address all women as Ms. unless it is otherwise stated. For example, Judy Barton, Nursing Unit Manager would be greeted as 'Dear Ms. Barton,'.

* Some married women choose to call themselves Mrs. and make this very clear. For instance, (Mrs) Sarah Jones would be greeted as 'Dear Mrs Jones,'

* You write a comma after the name of the recipient e.g. *Dear Ms Jones,*

* You **never** write 'Dear Mrs Susan,' or 'Dear Mr John,'

Full stop after Mr, Mrs or Dr?

Australia tends to follow British usage which differs from American usage.

The rules are as follows:

1. If the abbreviation ends with the same letter as the whole word, no full stop is used.

2. If the abbreviation ends with a letter which doesn't end the whole word, a full stop is used.

3. The invented title Ms has widely displaced Miss to describe a feminine form which does not indicate marital status. A full stop is not used.

Abbreviation	Whole word	Full stop or no full stop?
Mr	Mister	Dear Mr Jones,
Mrs	Mistress	Dear Mrs Jones,
Dr	Doctor	Dear Dr Jones,
Sr	Sister	Dear Sr Jones,
Prof.	Professor	Dear Prof. Jones,
Capt.	Captain	Dear Capt. Jones,
Ms	Ms	Dear Ms Jones,

How do you address a child in a letter?

A male child (up to around the age of 18) is referred to as 'Master'. There is no abbreviation:

Dear Master Jones,

A female child (up to around the age of 18) is referred to as 'Miss'. There is no abbreviation:

Dear Miss Jones,

What if you are not told the recipient's name?

If you are not told the name of the recipient, you need to use the fixed expression:

Dear Sir / Madam,

A note about 'dear'

When speaking, the expression 'dear' is used as a term of endearment. The expression is an old-fashioned term which is mostly used by older people these days. It is not generally considered appropriate for younger people to use.

For example, 'Would you like a piece of cake, dear?'

Look at these examples:

Name of the recipient in the task	How you write the salutation

Ms Edith Swinton	Dear Ms Swinton,
Mr Lawrence Suffolk	Dear Mr Suffolk,
(Mrs) Judith McNee	Dear Mrs McNee,
Sister Mary Martin-Brown	Dear Sr Martin-Brown,
Mr Peter Rodriguez	Dear Mr Rodriguez,
Ms Wendy Havelock	Dear Ms Havelock,
Dr Simon Platt	Dear Dr Platt,

Definitions relating to names

double-barrelled name	This is when a person uses the family name of both father and mother. It is not uncommon these days especially if a baby's parents are not married or if a baby's mother chooses to retain her maiden name. Both names are joined using a hyphen. E.g. Martin-Brown Use both names as one name.
maiden name	This is a woman's name when she is single – 'maiden' means 'young girl'.
surname	Also called *family name*. Used to be called *Christian Name* but this is not considered appropriate.
middle name	This is an extra name which parents sometimes give their children. It may be the name of a relative or grandparent.
nickname	A 'pet name' people like to be called by friends. It might be a shortened form of a name. E.g. 'Tommy' is a nickname for 'Thomas'.

Writing the recipient's address

The name and address of the recipient are written flush at the left side of the page. For example:

Ms Sarah Jones

Hillview Community Health Centre

15 Jackson St

Hillview   NSW   2654

These days we do not use a comma at the end of each line of the address. Look at the address above and notice how it is written:

Number of the house etc. + street name + abbreviation of the type of street.

Some common abbreviations are:

Ave	Avenue
Cnr	Corner
Cres	Crescent
Ln	Lane
Pde	Parade
Pway	Parkway
Rd	Road
St	Street

Writing the suburb and postcode

The second line is in the format:

Suburb + state + postcode (no commas in between)

You write the abbreviation of the suburb as below.

If the stimulus material only gives you the suburb and the postcode, just write that. If you know the state from the postcode, you can write it. For example, if you see a postcode starting with a 3, you may know that this is a postcode for Victoria.

Abbreviations of Australian states and territories:

ACT   Australian Capital Territory

NT   Northern Territory

NSW   New South Wales

Qld   Queensland

SA   South Australia

Tas   Tasmania

Vic   Victoria

WA   Western Australia

Note: In Australia each state has a postcode beginning with a number for the state e.g. All postcodes in NSW start with a 2. The American term 'zip code' has the same meaning as postcode.

Writing the date

The date format which is used in Australia and New Zealand is:

day + month + year   e.g. 10 September, 2013

You can also write the date:

10th September, 2013 (you say it '10th of September,2013)

You can use numbers only: 10/9/2013. However, using numbers has the potential to be confusing if you are not careful. If you accidentally use the American system of writing dates (month/day/year) it can be confusing. E.g.

10/9/2013 = 10 September, 2013 (Australia)

10/9/2013 = 9 October, 2013 (U.S)

Make sure you know the correct number forms.

Number	Ordinal numbers	Spoken
1	1st	first
2	2nd	second
3	3rd	third
4	4th	fourth
5	5th	fifth
6	6th	sixth
7	7th	seventh
8	8th	eighth
9	9th	ninth
10	10th	tenth
11	11th	eleventh
12	12th	twelfth

The spelling of the month

The month that many people misspell is February (don't miss the 'r')

The reference information

Write   Re: [name of the patient], [age]

' Re' means 'regarding' or 'referring to'.

This focuses the receiver of the letter on the content of the letter. It should focus you on the person you are writing about.

2. What is the reason for writing? Explain the main purpose of your letter at the start, e.g.

- discharge letter for a patient going home and needing nursing support
    - transfer letter for a patient going to a nursing home
    - discharge letter for a patient going home and needing follow-up care by their GP

Be clear about the level of urgency of your letter e.g.

- 'The patient will need to have an INR in two days' time'.

- 'The patient requires suture removal in a week'.

3. What treatment did the patient receive? Decide whether to use a time line sequence or a simple description.

4. What is the discharge plan? What new medication has been prescribed or what medication has been restarted? What physio has been started? What equipment has been supplied?

5. What complications did the patient suffer? Were there any abnormal events during the operation or in the post-operative period? What happened?

6. What are the post-op instructions? When will sutures or clips be removed? When does the patient need a dressing change? When does the patient need a blood test?

7. Closing - appropriate ending with appropriate signature.

What does a paragraph look like?

Generally a paragraph has one idea only. This may be:

- one point of a single idea with supporting evidence
- several points of a single idea

Paragraphs often start with a topic sentence, although it may be any sentence in the paragraph. The topic sentence should tell you what the paragraph is about. It should contain at least one key term. You can think of the topic sentence as a summary of the paragraph.

After the topic sentence you will need to develop the paragraph to support the main idea. In a paragraph of 35-40 words, you will probably add 2-3 sentences to support the topic sentence.

Some examples of supporting sentences:

- sentences which give examples
- sentences which add facts or figures
- sentences which use a study as an illustration
- sentences which define terms

1. Salutation

- Writing an address – no commas used at the end of each line

- Writing a date e.g. 4 September, 2013

- Brief statement of the patient's name and age e.g. Re: Mr Gerald Baker, aged 79

- Salutation – e.g. Dear Mr Brown, Dear Ms Smith, Dear Dr Green

2. What is the reason for writing?

1. What is happening today?

- Present continuous - Mr Baker is being discharged today.

- Present simple 'is for + noun' – Mr Baker is for discharge today.

2. Why was the patient in hospital?

- Past simple – Mr Baker underwent a left total hip replacement.

3. What is his current level of mobility?

- Present simple - He has good mobility and can walk along the ward using a wheelie walker.

3. What is the discharge plan? New medication or restarting previous medication

- Passive – 'He underwent (or He was recommenced) on aspirin 75mg daily.

What post-op care is needed?

- Present simple – He requires (or needs) daily dressings.

- 'is to + verb' – He is to undergo a series of range-of-motion exercises

4. What were the peri-operative complications?

- Past simple – He was disoriented

5. What are the post-op instructions?

- Future – He will have his staples removed on 21 September. He will have follow-up blood tests.

Control of linguistic features (grammar and cohesion)

Remember that most of your sentences will be quite simple so you can concentrate on writing clear and accurate sentences. You are not using descriptive language in most cases, you are passing on information and facts. It is better to write short accurate sentences rather than long confusing ones!

Review verb forms used to indicate present time (what the patient is doing now), past time (what happened to the patient in hospital) and future time (what needs to happen for the patient in the next days and weeks). The passive is also used quite frequently in formal writing. For example:

- Present time – Mr X is being discharged home today. Mrs Y is being transferred to you today.
- Past time – Mr X underwent a right knee arthroscopy. Mrs Y underwent cardiac monitoring in our unit over the past three days.
- Future time – Mr X will need to have his clips /sutures /staples removed on 5.4.2013. Mrs Y will need to have a FBC and INR three days after discharge. Mr X is for repeat MRSA swabbing next month.
- Passive – Mr X was commenced on Frusemide 40mg bd for fluid retention. Mrs Y was started on a programme of gentle exercise.

Make sure your verbs agree with the subject. You need to match a single noun with the third person singular verb form (there is, has, underwent, shows) and a plural noun with the third person plural with the third person plural form (there are, have, show) e.g.

- The X-ray shows a small area of consolidation in the right lung.
- There is no evidence of cancer in the liver.
- He has lived in the country all his life.

The ending of the letter

You can use a stock ending for your letter which is easy to learn and re-use. You are concluding the letter and making yourself available if the person needs more information. You can use sentences like:

Thank you for accepting this referral. Should you need more information please contact me.

Yours sincerely,   These days, 'Yours sincerely' (capital Y) is used rather than 'Yours faithfully'. Formerly, 'Yours faithfully' was used if you did not know the person you were writing to. 'Yours sincerely' was only used for friends. It is now quite acceptable to use 'Yours sincerely'.

[Your name and title] Your title will be found at the top of the stimulus material. E.g. 'You are a Registered Nurse on the Respiratory Unit at Mt Sinat Hospital.

2. OET Writing for Nurses: Starting and Ending the writing task.

The words in the beginning and ending of the referral letter do not count towards the 180 – 200 word limit. The setting out of the address, date and salutation are in a standard form. Once you know how to set out a letter, it is a matter of filling in information from the stimulus material.

The order of the initial set up is as follows:

1. Name of the person you are writing to – usually with the person's title e.g. Ms Susan Rodriguez

2. Title of the recipient – this is usually found at the end of the writing task e.g. Mr Tom Smith, Head Physiotherapist.

3. Address of the recipient – this should be written in two lines:

    Number of house/apartment + Street name + St/Rd/Ln etc.

    Suburb name + state + postcode

4. Leave a space

5. Date - you will often be asked to put in the date of the test e.g. [today's date].

    Use the Australian / NZ date format

6. Leave a space

7. Dear [salutation] – using correct format e.g. Dear Ms, Dear Mrs, Dear Dr + last name + comma

8. Leave a space

9. Reference information : Name of patient being referred and his/her age

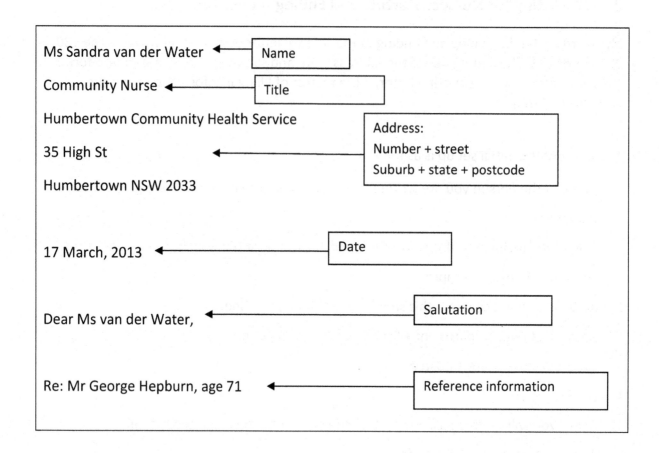

The date

Australian /New Zealand convention is the format:

day + month + year

e.g. 10 September, 2013

You can also use numbers only: 10/9/2013.

However, using numbers has the potential to be confusing if you are not careful. If you

accidentally use the American system of writing dates (month/day/year) it can be confusing.

E.g. Writing 11/9/2013 means 11th September, 2013 (Aus/NZ) but 9th November, 2013 (U.S)

It's best to stick with one convention only when writing a letter.

Also, when you refer to a month <u>within</u> the letter, always write the full word e.g.

'Mrs X has an appointment at the Cardiac Clinic next October.' (not 'next Oct')

Full stop after titles

Australia tends to follow British usage which differs from American usage.

The rules are as follows:

4. If the abbreviation ends with the same letter as the whole word, no full stop is used.

5. If the abbreviation ends with a letter which doesn't end the whole word, a full stop is used.

6. The invented title Ms has widely displaced Miss to describe a feminine form which does not indicate marital status. A full stop is not used.

Abbreviation	Whole word ends with the same letter as the abbreviation	Whole word does not end with the same letter as the abbreviation	Invented Title
Mr	Mister		
Mrs	Mistress		
Dr	Doctor		
Sr	Sister		
Prof.		Professor	
Capt.		Captain	
Ms			Ms

The difference between Australian / NZ style and US style

Australian / NZ style: Ms Jones, Mr Jones, Mrs Jones

US style: Ms. Jones, Mr. Jones, Mrs. Jones

Writing the address:

These days we do not use a comma at the end of each line of the address. Look at the address above and notice how it is written:

We write the address in the order:
Number of the flat / Number of the house etc. + street name + abbreviation of the type of street. E.g.
4/11 Hughes St (Flat 4, building number 11 in Hughes street)
6-8 Long Rd   (building 6 to 8 in Long Road)

Salutation

This is a section many people have difficulty with. In English, the convention is to address people as follows:

1. Addressing a friend – first names are used. E.g. Dear Susan, (Notice the comma after the name)

2. Addressing someone you do not know but whose name you know
– use Mr /Mrs/Miss/Ms + their last name e.g. Dear Mr Blogs, (Notice that there is a comma after the name)

3. Addressing someone you do not know and whose name you do not know – say
Dear Sir / Madam, (Notice the comma)

** **A common mistake is to use the person's first name with Mr /Mrs /Miss /Ms.** For example, 'Mr Bill' instead of 'Mr Smith' (the person's name is Mr Bill Smith). It is incorrect to do this.

*** Another mistake is to address a person you do not know as 'dear' e.g. 'Hello, dear'. The word 'dear' has several meanings. In the case of salutations, we use it:
1. to start a letter e.g. Dear Mr Smith / Mary / Sister Brown,
2. as an old-fashioned term of endearment. These days it is usually only the elderly who use this term. E.g. 'Hello, dear. How are you feeling?'

In writing a letter, you are using the phrase 'Dear _____,'

The ending of the letter

You can use a stock ending for your letter which is easy to learn and re-use. The idea is that you are concluding the letter and making yourself available if the person needs more information.

You can use sentences like:

Thank you for accepting this referral. Should you need more information please contact me.

The ending

Yours sincerely,

Virginia Allum

Charge Nurse

Bloomfield General Hospital

These days, 'Yours sincerely' (capital Y) is used rather than 'Yours faithfully'. Formerly, 'Yours faithfully' was used if you did not know the person you were writing to. 'Yours sincerely' was only used for friends. It is now quite acceptable to use 'Yours sincerely'.

[Your name and title] Your title will be found at the top of the stimulus material. E.g. 'You are a Registered Nurse on the Respiratory Unit at Mt Sinat Hospital....' The ending would be:

Yours sincerely,

Virginia Allum (put your name here)

Registered Nurse

Respiratory Unit Mt Sinat Hospital

3. OET Writing for Nurses - The outline of the referral letter

Name of recipient: [in the writing task, person you are writing to e.g. Ms Petra Simmonds]

Name of community centre /hospital /clinic/ hostel:

Address: [Note: Suburb   State   Postcode   e.g. Bundall Qld 4217

[leave a line]

Date: (day month year e.g. 17 January, 2014 or 17th January, 2014

[leave a line]

Dear [correct salutation] e.g. Dear Ms Brown,   [no full stop after Mr/Mrs. Comma after name)

Re: Mr Bill Brown, aged 82   [good idea to include age so it doesn't go in the letter]

[Paragraph 1: Why are you writing the letter?]
I am writing to refer Mr X for ongoing care and support. Mr X was admitted to the hospital with ...... / after a (heart attack /car accident / hypoglycaemic attack / dog bite. He suffers from   ....

[Paragraph 2: What treatment in hospital?]
During hospitalisation, he underwent .... / received treatment for .../ was assessed for... He was also reviewed by the physio /occupational therapist / dietician and started an exercise programme /weight loss programme / Quit Smoking programme.

[Paragraph 3: What complication occurred?]
Whilst in hospital, Mr X had an episode of chest pain which was treated with GTN spray/developed a wound infection / chest infection which has now resolved.

[Paragraph 4: What do you want the nurse at the hostel to do? (discharge plan)]

Could you please.... Would you also..... Please ...... It would also be beneficial if you could.... Finally, could you .....

Closing sentence. (stock sentence e.g. Should you require any further details, please feel free to contact me)

Yours sincerely,

[your name]

[title e.g. Registered Nurse /Charge Nurse]

7. OET Writing - Know your prepositions

1.Prep - with

admit with   He was admitted with back pain and decreasing mobility.

diagnose with + noun   She was diagnosed with breast cancer six months ago.

transfer with   He transfers from bed to chair with a walking frame.

treat with   Mrs Greene was treated with a course of radiotherapy.

mobilise with   Mr Black mobilises with a stick.

supervise with   She will need to be supervised with her medication.

present with   Mr Grey presented with epigastric pain and nausea.

comply with   Unfortunately, she does not comply with her medication and often skips a dose.

liaise with   Please liaise with Mr Browne's GP regarding his regular blood tests.

cope with   She finds it difficult to cope with her mother's aggression.

need assistance with + gerund   He needs assistance with dressing and general hygiene.

difficulty with + gerund   She has difficulty with communication because of the stroke.

appointment with (doctor/dietician) at the Outpatient Clinic/Diabetes Clinic   Mr Rose has an appointment with the Vascular Clinic on June 6.

associated with   He has rib pain associated with breathing in and out.

independent with ADLs   Miss Redford is independent with her ADLs.

Some examples using verb + with

He was admitted with a fractured left tibia and fibula.

His urinary tract infection was treated with a course of antibiotics.

She mobilises with a wheelie walker.

She is being transferred with a back slab in situ.

He needs supervision with his medications.

She was diagnosed with type 1 diabetes.

He presented to hospital with increasing shortness of breath

in situ - in place e.g. 'a cannula in situ' means that the patient has an intravenous cannula inserted.

2. Prep - from

suffer from

be in remission from

discharge from hospital

discharge from a wound

estranged from

withdraw from a drug

pastoral care from

3. Prep - on

start on

commence on

patient education on + noun

dependent on heroin

4. Prep – of

complain of

an application of

a diagnosis of

assessment of

monitoring of

production of   production of thick sputum

episode of   several episodes of loose stool

symptoms of

X-ray/CT/MRI of

management of

capable of

accepting of the need for hospitalisation

5. Prep - for

provide support for

6. Prep - to

refer to

allergic to

sensitive to

spread to

advise to   advise to quit smoking

present to + date   she presented to me on May 3

prompt to / needs prompting to

be addicted to

orient to   orient him to his environment

relating to

secondary to

give support to

7. Prep - by

aggravate by

made worse by

relieve by

improved by

soothed by

8. Prep - towards

aggressive towards

Some forms are different for verbs and noun forms. Complete the table with the variations (verb form and noun form)

verb	noun
diagnose with	a diagnosis of

Some examples

Treatment received

- Chest infection treated with antibiotics and chest physio.

Mr Turner was treated for a chest infection with antibiotics and chest physio.

Mr Turner was admitted with a productive cough which was treated with antibiotics and chest physio.

Whilst in hospital, Mr Turner's chest infection was treated with antibiotics as well as chest physio.

- Frusemide dose increased from mane to bd.

Mr Turner's Frusemide dose was increased to twice a day to better manage his oedema.

The oedema in Mr Turner's lower legs was managed with an increased dose of Frusemide.

Mr Turner was also treated for oedema and now takes Frusemide twice a day.

- Started nutritional supplements and monitoring by hospital dietician

Mr Turner's decreasing weight and loss of appetite was reviewed by the dietician. He has been started on nutritional supplements and ongoing review.

Mr Turner has been seen by the dietician and started on nutritional supplements to assist with his recent weight loss.

Mr Turner has lost weight and was commenced on nutritional supplements.

Other expressions to describe symptoms

became hypotensive / hypertensive / hypothermic/ tachycardic

became confused / disoriented / aggressive/depressed /unresponsive/uncooperative

became hyponatraemic /hypocalaemic / anaemic

developed a pressure ulcer / chest infection/wound infection

complained of chest pain / angina / numbness and tingling in the fingers / chest tightness

developed reduced renal function/reduced cardiac output

exhibited poor glycaemic control/fluctuating bgls

had a hypoglycaemic attack

had a fall/sustained bruising from a fall/ sustained a fractured arm from a fall

suffered from bouts of diarrhoea and vomiting/ episodes of urinary / faecal / double

incontinence / constipation /faecal overflow /faecal impaction

Unfortunately, Mr Browne had a fall on March 26 and sustained considerable bruising to his left arm. He was X-rayed and found to have a very small crack on his ulna which fortunately only required immobilisation with a collar and cuff.

During her hospitalisation Mrs Redfern became increasing confused and uncooperative. Blood tests revealed that she had become hyponatraemic as a result of diuretic use. She responded well to a one litre fluid restriction and the stopping of her diuretics. She has been started on an alternative diuretic and does not require fluid restriction any more.

Mr Blackmore developed a wound infection whilst in hospital. The wound is located on his left hip and became infected during frequent episodes of faecal incontinence. Wound management has therefore been extremely difficult, however, frequent pad checks and prompt cleaning of faecal matter have made a difference.

Whilst on our ward, Mr White suffered from three episodes of diarrhoea and vomiting and was isolated in a side room. He has had no further episodes for the past 48 hours and is therefore fit for discharge.

During her stay in hospital, Mrs Gold's glycaemic control was noted to be poor. She had a hypoglycaemic attack (bgl of 1.7) two days ago which she claims is unusual. It was noted that she had missed her last appointment at the Diabetes Clinic as she claimed that she was 'managing fine without their help.'

8. Collocations

You will start to notice that you are using some expressions a lot. It's important to learn the expressions 'together'. For example, you say 'I am referring Mr Bloggs **to** your care'. The ability to use the correct expression makes your work grammatically correct and makes it sound fluent.

If you look at the table below you can see verbs with their corresponding preposition. It's a good idea to make a page in your notebook and add to it as you hear more. Carry the notebook around with you and keep looking at it. You will find that you start hearing the expressions more and more. Add more expressions that you hear.

Table 1: verb + preposition	Examples
refer to	Mr Smith has been referred to the Diabetic Clinic.
discharge to	discharge to the care of his wife
transfer to	transfer to a Nursing Home
respond to	respond well to treatment no response to painful stimulus She does not respond to painful stimuli.
be sensitive to (emotional and physical)	1. She's sensitive to soap. (a physical thing) 2. She's sensitive to criticism.(an emotional thing)
be allergic to	He is allergic to penicillin.
bend over backwards to	He bent over backwards to help her (took a lot of trouble to help her)
complain of	He was complaining of back and flank pain. (Note: different meaning in the medical sense. Complain of = say you have a symptom)

episode of	episode of chest pain / diarrhoea/vomiting Note: many diseases and conditions are Uncountable Nouns (e.g. asthma, angina, hypertension, arthritis, burns etc.). So, if you want to talk about 'more than one' you have to add a 'counting phrase'. You also use 'episode of' to describe a condition that lasts a length of time. E.g. He has only had one episode of angina. (it lasted a length of time) You would not use 'episode of' to describe a cut. E.g. He cut himself. He has a cut on his leg. A cut is a single action not a long activity.
symptoms of	with the symptoms of headache, earache and vertigo
removal of (excision)	removal of dead skin
insertion of (anything that goes into the body)	insertion of a fistula
excision of	excision of skin tag
sense of	have a sense of fulfilment
feelings of	He suffers from feelings of hopelessness.
amount of	small / moderate/large amount of wound discharge
be afraid of	He is afraid of losing his hair.
take advantage of	You need to take advantage of the services at the hospital.
loss of consciousness (to lose consciousness)	There was no loss of consciousness. (Note: abbreviation is LOC) He did not lose consciousness.
inflammation of (suffix –itis)	inflammation of surrounding tissue
associate with	The pain is associated with movement.

present with	present with the symptoms of chest pain and hypertension.
treat with	treat with anti-inflammatories
contact with	He has had contact with a child with whooping cough.
consult with	consult with a colleague about something
communicate with	communicate with your case manager
be pleased with	I am pleased with your progress.
get on with something	I'm going to get on with your dressing now.
get along with someone	She doesn't get along with her husband at all.
keep up with something	You need to keep up with the treatment for it to work.
take it up with someone	You should take that up with your GP. (= discuss it)
review by	The X-ray was reviewed by the radiologist yesterday.
assess by	The wound has been assessed by the Tissue Viability Nurse.
started / commenced on	started / commenced on a diuretic (or any medication) / a Quit Smoking programme.
choke on	He was choking on a piece of bread.
room for	There's no room for complacency. (fixed expression) = We must not sit back and do nothing.

fill somebody in about	Can you fill me in about Mrs Smith? (Can you tell me what has been happening with Mrs Smith?)
break out in	She broke out in a rash.
result in	Smoking cigarettes may result in breathlessness and increased risk of chest infection.

6. OET GRAMMAR – VERBS WITH INFINITIVE 'TO' OR GERUND 'ING'

Useful resources:

www.learnenglish.de/grammar/verbsgerundinf.html

www.englishclub.com/grammar/verbs-m_infinitive-ing.htm

Verbs are divided into four basic groups:

1. verbs which only take the infinitive ('to')

2. verbs which only take the gerund ('ing')

3. verbs which take either infinitive or gerund with **no** change of meaning

4. verbs which take either infinitive or gerund with **a** change of meaning.

1. The infinitive

* After certain verbs

* After **adjectives** e.g.

I was disappointed /sad /relieved to hear about the news.

I am glad / happy / pleased to know that your wound is healing.

He was surprised to learn about the new treatment.

* After **too + adjective**:

The coffee **too hot** to drink.

* After **adjective + enough**:

He is not **strong enough** to walk by himself.

2. The gerund

* After certain verbs

* After verbs with a preposition

3. Verbs with little change in meaning
begin   continue   hate   intend   like   love   neglect   prefer   propose   start   try

4. Verbs with a change in meaning
forget   remember   stop

Verbs which take the infinitive	
agree	He agreed to join the Quit Smoking Programme.
allow (someone)	I'm sorry but I can't allow **you** to see her at the moment.
can't afford	I can't afford to continue the treatment.
choose	I chose to work in ICU because I like a challenge.
decide	He decided to have the knee replacement in the end.
encourage (someone)	I encouraged **him** to cut down on smoking.
expect	You should expect to feel better in a week.
help (someone)	I'll help **you** to get dressed.
hope	I hope to be able to run again in a month's time.
learn	You'll learn to use the walking frame with the physio.
manage	I managed to stop the bleeding after about ten minutes.
mean	I meant to change the dressing this morning but I didn't have time.
need	You need to take the tablets twice a day.
neglect	He neglected to tell the doctor about his weight loss.
offer	The nutritionist offered to speak to Mrs Smith about her new diet.
pretend	She only pretended to take the medication.
promise	He promised to stop using cannabis.
refuse	He refused to take his 2 o'clock meds.
train (someone)	The Stoma Therapist will train **her** to change the pouch herself.
want	I want to ask you some questions about the injury.
would like	I would like to speak to you about the pain you've been having.

Verbs which only take the gerund (-ing)	
avoid	You should avoid getting the dressing wet.
dislike	He dislikes eating green vegetables.
don't mind	I don't mind coming back in a few minutes.
enjoy	Do you enjoy walking or swimming?
finish	I've finished doing the dressing now.
give up	She gave up eating meat last year.
leave without	He left without saying goodbye.
look forward to	I'm looking forward to speaking to the physio about the exercises.
practise	You'll have to practise using the crutches.

Verbs which take infinitive or gerund – little or no change in meaning	
begin	He began to feel better after the operation.
	He began feeling better after the operation.
start	It start to hurt this afternoon.
	It start hurting this afternoon.
continue	You should continue to take the tablets until they are finished.
	You should continue taking the tablets until they are finished.
hate	She hates to have to get up early in the morning.
	She hates having to get up early in the morning.
love	She loves to hear from her family.
	She loves hearing from her family.
try	Why don't you try to walk a little each day.
	Why don't you try walking a little each day.

Verbs which take infinitive or gerund - change in meaning	
forget to	I forgot to give the antibiotic. (I didn't give it)
forget + gerund	I forgot giving the antibiotic. (I gave it but didn't remember that I had given it.)
go on to (went on to)	He went on to develop a skin disease. (He developed a skin disease later.)
go on +gerund (went on + gerund)	He went on hitting the table. (He continued to hit the table.)
like to	I like to clean my hands with alcohol gel. (I like alcohol gel rather than soap and water.)
like + gerund	I like cleaning my hands with alcohol gel. (I like the choice of alcohol gel.)
prefer to	I prefer to use tape to secure the dressing. (if there is a choice of tape or something else)
prefer + gerund	I prefer using tape to secure the dressing. (that's what I prefer to use in general.)
remember to	I remembered to phone for an appointment. (I knew that I had to make an appointment.)
remember + gerund	I remembered phoning for an appointment. (I knew that I had made the appointment)
regret to	I regret to tell you that the clinic has closed. (I am sorry to tell you that the clinic has closed.)
regret + ing	She regretted taking the tablets. (She was sorry that she had taken the tablets.
stop to	He stopped to speak to Mrs Smith during his Rounds. (He was in the middle of doing Rounds on the ward and he stopped and had a conversation with Mrs Smith.)
stop + gerund	He stopped smoking last week. (He had his last cigarette last week.)

7. OET Writing: Using a hyphen with numbers

Rule 1: If you write out a number from 21 – 99, you need to separate the numbers using a hyphen.

0	zero, nought	10	ten	100	hundred	1000	thousand
1	one	11	eleven				
2	two	12	twelve	20	twenty	21	twenty-one
3	three	13	thirteen	30	thirty	32	thirty-two
4	four	14	fourteen	40	**forty**	43	forty-three
5	five	15	fifteen	50	fifty	54	fifty-four
6	six	16	sixteen	60	sixty	65	sixty-five
7	seven	17	seventeen	70	seventy	76	seventy-six
8	eight	18	eighteen	80	eighty	87	eighty-seven
9	nine	19	nineteen	90	ninety	98	ninety-eight

Use a hyphen when you write out a fraction. For example:

⅔   two-thirds

⅕   one-fifth

¾   three-quarters

⅝   five-eighths

Rule 2: When a number is used to make an adjective, we add a hyphen between the number and words. This is because the words work together as a single adjective. The hyphens make the words clear.

1. We'll have a one-hour meeting about his case. but The meeting will last one hour.

2. He came into hospital after a two-week illness. but The illness lasted two weeks.

3. Jimmy is a five-year-old with a lot of energy. but Jimmy is five years old.

4. Tomorrow you'll do a ten-minute stress test. but The stress test lasts ten minutes.

* Look at example 1. 'We'll have a one-hour meeting about his case.' If I had written 'We'll have a one hour meeting about his case.', it may have meant ' We are only having one meeting (lasting an hour) about this case. No further meetings'.

* Look at examples 2 and 3. Notice that we say:

2. a two-week illness ('week' is singular) but The illness lasted two weeks.('weeks' is plural)

3. a five-year-old ('year' is singular) but Jimmy is five years old. ('years' is plural)

Rule 3: A hyphen can be used to indicate a range of numbers. For example, from one date to another date. If you use the words ' from' .... 'to' , you should not use a hyphen.

He suffered from chronic bronchitis 1990 – 1995.

He suffered from chronic bronchitis from 1990 to 1995.

Examples:

1a   He has gained five kilos since June.

1b   He had a five-kilo weight gain since June.

2a   The shifts on this unit are 12 hours long.

2b   They are 12-hour shifts on this unit.

3a   He is on 24-hour monitoring at the moment.

3b   The monitor is undertaken over 24 hours.

7.   Starting an OET speaking for nurses role play

After you have looked at the tasks on your role play, you should have an idea of the language the interviewer will be expecting to hear from you. In other words, what is the purpose of the role play.

Is it :

- to give information or explain treatment
- to persuade the patient to do something or not to do something
- to empathise with the patient
- to give advice

You should be able to draw on some expressions which you have practised beforehand. But starting the role play is sometimes difficult. In authentic conversations, you will have been taught to ask open questions to encourage the patient to talk. The OET asks you to do this while doing most of the talking yourself.

There are two paths the conversation may take. The first possibility is that you will start the conversation. The second possibility is that the 'patient' will start it off. Remember that you won't have the benefit of seeing the patient's role card so it will be guess work in the beginning.

The role play cards contain around 4 tasks for you to cover. The first task is the cue for the start of the role play. The most common is a 'Find out about..' task. Some examples are:

Ask about... or Find out about....

1. Scurvy: Ask Jake about his class room behaviour. Ask detailed questions about his diet and lifestyle.

2. Bedwetting: Find out the out the frequency of bedwetting and if there are any other concerns.

3. Young child with epilepsy: Find out as much as you can about the boy's condition.

4. Immunisation: Find out exactly what the patient's concerns are.

5. Child with burns: Find out as much as you can about the accident and subsequent treatment of the burns.

6. Parkinson's Disease: Find out what the patient is having difficulty with.

7. Head injury: Find out as much as you can about the details of the patient's accident and any symptoms.

8. Appendectomy: Find out as much as you can about the details of the patient's accident and any symptoms.

Other 'first tasks' are:

Give the patient information about....
- Baby with jaundice: Give the patient information and advice on the condition.
- Advice on hip replacement surgery: Focus on the positive aspect of the surgery
- Mother with stroke: Explain why you are monitoring the patient.

Try to persuade....
- Resident in Nursing Home: Try to persuade the resident to take the medication

Discuss patient concerns
- Child with meningitis: Discuss the parents' worries

Let's look at the ' 'find out about...' task. Before I start, I'll go through the two conversation possibilities. I mentioned the role play that you, the nurse, starts.

If you are starting the conversation, it's quite good to introduce yourself and explain your position in the ward or community centre. You'll find out the information about this on the role play card. Look at the 'Setting' for some direction e.g. Hello, Mrs Smith. My name's Virginia. I'm a Registered Nurse on this ward.

If the patient starts the conversation, it may sound a little strange to introduce yourself as it may be accepted that this has already happened. As the patient starts talking, use Active Listening techniques to indicate that you are paying attention. You'll remember that this is:

- nodding your head
- saying 'Uh huh', 'Oh right' and 'Mm'
- smiling

Can you tell me about?

Then, you can look at the 'find out about' question, that is, why the patient is talking to you. In order to ask an open question, you'll use 'Can you tell me about …?' or 'Can you tell me how long…?' 'Can you tell me what…?'

Be careful with 'Can you tell me about…' as it must be followed by a noun. Review these forms:

'Can you tell me about the pain?

'Can you tell me about your leg ulcer?

The verb in a Can you tell me where/what/who ….? is in reverse.

Where **did** you **take** your son? → Can you tell me where you **took** your son?

What medication **do you take**? → Can you tell me what medication **you take**?

What **is** your name? → Can you tell me what your name **is?**

The difference between open and closed questions

Look at these examples from the bedwetting role play:

Closed: How often does he wet the bed? – you'd expect the patient to say 'Every night' or 'He wets the bed all the time'.

Closed: Can you tell me how often he wets the bed? – similar to the previous question

Open: Can you tell me about his bedwetting? – Notice that I had to use a noun form (gerund)

Here are some more examples:

What caused your daughter's injury? - **closed**

Can you tell me what caused your daughter's injury? - **closed**

Can you tell me about your daughter's injury? – **open** question

A variation is 'Can you tell me a bit more about your daughter's injury?'

If you want to use a verb with the 'Can you tell me about' expression, you need to add a 'wh' question word onto it, e.g.

Can you tell me more about **what** happened to your daughter?

Can you tell me a bit more about **how often** your son has this problem?

Can you tell me a bit more about **why** you are concerned?

Notice that the order of words changes in these questions:

How often **does** your son **have** this problem? becomes

'Can you tell me a bit more about how often your son **has** this problem?'

Why **are you** concerned? becomes

Can you tell me a bit more about why **you are** concerned?

Using the wrong order of words is a common mistake. As the 'Can you tell me about...?' question will be one of the expressions you'll use a lot, you must get it right.

Can you tell me about: the placement of prepositions

Another point is the placement of prepositions in a question. If you are starting the conversation and are unsure of the reason for the patient's visit, you may ask:

- Can you tell me what you are concerned about?

- Can you tell me what you are worried about?

- Can you tell me what you have difficulty with?

- Can you tell me what you have problems with?

It's a good idea to make a list of verbs with their corresponding prepositions so you can use them confidently.

Some examples are:

treat with

present with (symptoms)

complain of

It's also a good idea to make a note of idioms and common expressions, e.g.

catch your breath

lose your voice

chew your fingernails -

clear your throat

8. OET SPEAKING – THE STRUCTURE OF THE ROLE PLAY

Role plays in the OET Speaking test are designed to be like conversations you might have with patients or patients' relatives. Remember that you do not need to describe complex procedures or have extensive medical knowledge.

What you do have to do is to communicate information in everyday terms to a member of the public who probably has limited medical knowledge. The speaking test relates to your profession so you need to think about the sorts of things you are likely to have to communicate. What are the common conditions in your profession? For example,

Podiatry - diabetes and foot care / tinea or athlete's foot / use of orthotics.
Speech pathology – dysphagia/ speech difficulties /stroke rehabilitation
Radiography – radiology tests / fear of claustrophobia e.g. in an MRI / risk of overexposure to radiation
Dietetics – weight loss /obesity / nutrition in the elderly / nutritional deficiencies
Occupational Therapy – mobility aids /home assessment / home modification

Each role play lasts 5 minutes. You will find that the tasks on the role play card guide you in the role play. Look at this basic plan for a role play:

1. Introduce yourself and explain your role.

2. Find out more about the problem.

3. Explain the condition / a test / a procedure / a new medication.

4. Give advice or make suggestions.

5. Use other communication strategies e.g. reassuring, reinforcing the importance of doing something, empathising.

6. Round the conversation off.

Generally, most role plays focus on finding out about a problem and then explaining what needs to happen. If you look at a few examples of role plays you will notice that most start with a 'find out more about' task. This is where you ask the patient to explain what is happening or what the problem is. For example, 'Can you tell me a bit more about the problem?', 'Can you tell me what's been happening lately?'

This task gives you the opportunity to do a few more things.

* You can display some non-verbal communication like nodding your head to indicate that you understand. You could use some 'listening noises' like 'Mm', 'OK,I see.' This indicates that you are actively listening to the other person.

*You could also confirm understanding by summarising: 'So, what you're saying is that you've been having trouble sleeping for a while now. You've put on a bit of weight and your wife says that you snore at night. Is that right?'

The next thing you will do is give an explanation about something. It may be a condition e.g. ' I'll explain what happens when you have a stroke. Sometimes blood flow to the brain is blocked. This means that parts of your brain don't get enough oxygen and this results in a stroke.'

It's a good idea to spend some time preparing this part of the role play before the test. Make sure you are able to explain common conditions which you come across in your profession in simple terms. Keep in mind that this is not a medical test – it is a test of your language ability. When you explain something, only use a few sentences and keep to everyday language if possible.

You may also be asked to display some more complex communication strategies, like giving advice, making suggestions, reassuring or empathising. In giving advice, you need to consider 'softeners' and softer expressions. For example, if you are giving advice it is better to say:

'It would be a good idea to lose some weight'.

'It would help a lot if you could exercise a bit more.'

rather than:

'You should lose some weight' or 'You should exercise more.'

'Softeners' like 'just' are also useful when giving advice. For example, 'I'll just explain about the MRI so you understand what will happen tomorrow.'

Finally, try to anticipate what the interlocutor may do, e.g.

* be difficult and refuse to take advice e.g. a young patient who wants to go home after having a baby and doesn't want to wait for blood test results.

* be reluctant to follow treatment e.g. woman who can't see the point of having dye in her eye to check it.

* be defensive e.g. about a dietician asking about your eating habits.

9. OET SPEAKING FOR NURSES: Reassuring a patient

Even though reassuring patients is a very common task for nurses and doctors, there has been very little research on how to give reassurance. It is usually understood that patients who receive no reassurance or ineffective reassurance do not recover as well as patients who receive positive and realistic reassurance. Nurses often use the phrase 'patient reassured' in the patient notes but this can sometimes mean no more than a pat on the arm and a clichéd expression.

When you reassure a patient you need to acknowledge first that you understand why they are upset or worried. If you don't so this, it may seem that you are 'fobbing them off' with excuses. This is an example of a communication block. Effectively, you give the listener the idea that you are too busy to listen or not interested.

Some patients need reassurance about issues that are sensitive e.g. a parent's guilt about a child who has sustained a burn or who has swallowed poison. It's important for patients to feel that you are not judging them and are not embarrassed by their concerns.

Remember that when you reassure a patient you must not include assurances that 'everything will be all right.' Role plays where this is particularly relevant are ones which deal with a possible diagnosis of cancer (e.g. a woman waiting for a biopsy result) or a possible admission to a Nursing Home (e.g. an elderly person who is struggling to cope at home).

What <u>not</u> to say:

'Don't worry. It will be OK.' (How do you know that?)

' Things always turn out in the end.' (But maybe they don't turn out in a satisfactory way)

'We are only sent as much as we can cope with.' (Perhaps but many people are unable to cope well if they are already under stress)

'Everything will be fine, you'll see.' (Fine for whom and if it isn't?)

'It's only a small procedure; nothing to worry about' (But it may be to the patient)

Nurses who dismiss a patient's concerns with a clichéd reassurance ('Don't worry. It will be OK') actually increase the patient's stress and anxiety levels. They also damage the trust between nurse and patient which may be difficult to rebuild.

The steps you take to reassure a patient

First, acknowledge the patient's concerns by using statements such as:

I can see that you are upset about this.

I can understand why you are concerned.

I appreciate that this has been very frightening for you.

I do understand that you are nervous about the operation. (You need to stress the word 'do' in this case)

Then, move on to the reassurance part. You need to reassure the patient by providing information, explaining that his/her concerns are natural or by reinforcing that the patient has taken the correct action. Remember that if you are giving a patient information, be sensitive to the amount of information they are able to take in. Confirm understanding every so often.

Make sure your verbal reassurance (the words) matches your non-verbal reassurance (your body language). It is important that your verbal and non-verbal reassurances are consistent with your actions (and the later actions of other healthcare practitioners). In other words, if you reassure a patient that 'all is well' but then say that the patient needs a blood test 'to check that everything is OK' – the patient will feel confused and not reassured at all.

Finally, be conscious of the fact that you will probably not be able to reassure a highly anxious patient. It is therefore not recommended that you try to reassure a patient who is already anxious. Other communication strategies are more appropriate.

Examples of statements used to reassure:

1. Providing information

I do understand that you are nervous about the operation. **I'll explain exactly what is going to happen tomorrow so you will know what to expect. Most people feel relieved if they know what to expect before an operation.**

2. Explaining that the concerns are natural

(I can see that you are upset about this.) **Actually, it's quite normal to have some concerns before you start the treatment. Would you like to talk to about it with me now?**

3. Reinforcing that the patient has taken the correct action

I can see that you are upset about this. **You did the right thing by bringing your husband into hospital as quickly as you did.**

Using expressions like 'Don't worry'

Use expressions like 'Don't worry', 'That's all right', 'That's OK' with care. If you don't embed the expressions they can sound like clichés or overused phrases that make it seem as though you are not interested in what your patient is saying. You can embed the expressions like this:

That's OK. I can see that you are upset about this. Actually, it's quite normal to have some concerns before you start the treatment. Would you like to talk to about it with me now?

I can see that you are upset about this. **Don't worry.** You did the right thing by bringing your husband into hospital as quickly as you did.

I <u>do</u> understand that you are nervous about the operation. **That's all right.** I'll explain exactly what is going to happen tomorrow so you will know what to expect. Most people feel relieved if they know what to expect before an operation.

Some literature on the topic

'Effective reassurance in primary care pain patients' from

http://www.paraplegie.ch/files/pdf3/Pincus1.pdf

'Reducing anxiety in elective surgical patients'

http://www.nursingtimes.net/nursing-practice/clinical-zones/perioperative-care/reducing-anxiety-in-elective-surgical-patients/5024376.article

'Reassurance: What Is It and Does It Work?'

http://www.mckenzieinstitute.co.uk/forms/Presentations/MIMDTP-Reassurance.pdf

10. OET SPEAKING FOR NURSES – CONVERSATION STRATEGIES

Strategies to use during a role play

During the speaking test, you have to make sure that you are in control of the conversation. You are expected to start things off and to maintain the flow of the conversation. In the real world, of course, you would be trying to encourage the patient to speak as much as possible. You would make sure that your conversations were patient-centred not nurse-centred.

You would ask open questions to get the person to talk more. During the OET speaking test, you need to be doing the talking most of the time. You still need to ask open questions but you also have to ensure that you display your communication ability.

Keep in mind that the interviewer and the assessors want to see how well you can communicate. The assessors will listen to the tape of your conversation afterwards and mark your performance. Correct grammar is important but sounding natural and developing a rapport with your 'patient' may be just as important. The sort of skills you need to show are:

1. introducing yourself and opening the conversation

2. asking open questions to encourage the patient to speak

3. taking turns in the conversation

4. summarising what you have said or what the 'patient' says

5. encouraging the 'patient' to change or try something

6. closing the conversation

Plan out the timing of the conversation. You have five minutes for each role play. You could plan it out like this:

<1 min   Introduce yourself and say what your title is. Here are some examples:

1. Hello, I'm Virginia. I'm the Registered Nurse looking after you today. – the role play is set in a hospital ward.

2. Hello, thanks for coming in today. I'm Virginia, one of the Registered Nurses at this clinic. – the role play is set at a Community Medical Centre.

3. Hello, I'm Virginia, the School Nurse. Thanks for coming to see me.- the role play is set in a school.

3-4 mins - go through the tasks on your role play card. Notice that there are often two issues per role play. Both issues often relate to each other.

There are usually four tasks on each card. One may be 'Find out more about …' – this is the beginning of the conversation where you hear what the problem is. Then, perhaps an 'Explain about x disease and its treatment' – you will talk about the kind of disease it is, how it may affect the patient and how it is treated.

What if I don't know anything about the disease on the role play card?

Remember that the role play is a language test. If you don't know what the disease is, describe any disease in general terms. E.g.

'I'll just explain a bit about the condition. It can be quite a serious condition if you don't look after yourself. You'll have some tests first to check your blood and possibly also a scan. The doctor will talk to you about that a bit later. I will explain everything about the tablets you'll be taking after you have the tests.' – as you can see, this could be any illness!

You can explain medication in general terms as well – 'The tablets you are going to take make you feel a little sick if you take them on an empty stomach. It's a good idea to take them with a meal or a dry biscuit.'

Practise the sort of language you would use to describe a disease or condition before you do the test. It's a good idea to learn the phrases you will use, e.g. 'take the whole course of antibiotics'.

You won't know what direction the 'patient' is going to take the conversation but you can assume that the 'patient' will try to be a bit difficult.

Some of the things a 'patient' may do:

1. The 'patient' keeps talking, may be upset about something that has happened – you need to politely 'jump in': e.g.

'Can I just interrupt you for a minute? I'd like to make sure that I understand what you are saying.'
'Can I just stop you now? I want to check that I understand correctly.'

Then, you can summarise what the 'patient' says to confirm that you understand. E.g.
'So, what you said was that you were walking on the street, then you fell over a rock and injured yourself.' Try to confirm understanding using steps.

2. The 'patient' won't say much. You are going to have to encourage him or her to open up. Ask open questions as often as you can, e.g.

'Can you tell me a bit more about what happened?'
'Can you explain again what happened?'

If the 'patient' still answers with one word or two, you can summarise what was said, e.g.
'I see. So you are saying that........'
'OK. So you told me that....'
You could also empathise with the 'patient' if this is relevant, e.g.
'I imagine that must have been very difficult for you.'
' That must have been very upsetting.'

3. The 'patient' tries to get you off track.

   You may be trying to explain something when the 'patient' tries to move the conversation in another direction. You will have to politely redirect the 'patient' where you want the conversation to go. E.g.
 'I can talk about that in a little while. Can we just get back to what we were talking about first.'
'Can I stop you there, please? I can see that you are upset about that. I will explain about that in a minute.'

4. The 'patient' is uncooperative – won't follow your advice.

In this case, you need to negotiate with your 'patient'. Some of the situations may be:

a teenager has scurvy but doesn't like fruit and vegetables.

an elderly gentleman refuses to have new tablets because they are the wrong colour.

a young mother insists on taking her baby home even though the baby is jaundiced.

You can use expressions such as:

'Would you be willing to try eating more oranges.'

'Would you be willing to wait until the blood results come back?'

'Could you just wait for a few minutes while I check your results?'

1 min - Closing the conversation.

If you have time, summarise the conversation. You can say:

'OK. We've talked about x, y, z.'

'Just to go over what we talked about...'

Then, you can suggest that the 'patient' may like to read a leaflet about the problem:

'I have a leaflet here which will explain a bit more about burns/scurvy/IBS etc. There's a number on the back which you can call for more information.'

'I'll give you this leaflet to read. Call me if you have any more questions after you've read it.'

Or, you can ask if the 'patient' has any questions he or she would like to ask.

'Do you have any questions you'd like to ask?'

'Is there anything else you'd like to ask?'

11. OET SPEAKING – PREDICTING VOCABULARY

The speaking role plays relate to common health topics. You will not be expected to discuss unusual medical cases – this is a test of your ability to communicate. Despite this, you will need a knowledge of some medical terms and their everyday equivalents. Remember that you may have to explain the condition to your 'patient'. Look at the list below of topics which you may come across and think about the vocabulary you may need to talk about the topics.

Alzheimer's disease

Asthma - asthma attack

Broken Bones (e.g. broken hip, broken arm etc)

Burns e.g. in children

Chicken Pox

High cholesterol levels

Diabetes e.g. foot care (podiatry) or poor blood glucose control

Discharge of an aged patient or transfer back to a Nursing Home or hostel

Eczema

Epilepsy - concerns by a grandparent/parent, fits

Fear of surgery e.g. appendectomy

Head Lice

Infection - wound care

Immunisation

Jaundice in newborns

Medication change – in the elderly

Myocardial Infarction – concerns about aftercare

Palliative care - pain and symptom control

Poor nutrition – anorexia nervosa, scurvy, the elderly

Pneumonia – physio, smoking advice

Urinary tract infection - antibiotics

Some vocab suggestions.

Build up your own glossary of terms for the most common health topics. For example,

1. **Alzheimer's Disease**	short term memory loss (STM loss)	Being unable to remember events which happened a short while ago.
	memory lapse / lapse of memory	Forgetting something but usually only for a short time, then remembering it.
	become forgetful	become increasingly unable to remember, usually daily activities.
	dementia	condition related to decline in brain function
	mood swing	changes in personality, usually sudden and without any reason.
	confusion /be confused become muddled	
	challenging behaviour	
	wandering	
	disorientation / be disoriented	

Showcase your ability to communicate!

Try to view role plays as an opportunity to show off your communication skills. Each role play is designed to allow you to display the sort of language functions you will need to use to conduct a conversation.

There are several functions which will be used repeatedly in many different situations. For instance, being able to formulate questions is essential so it is a good idea to predict the sort of questions you may be asking.

For example, in order to **find out more about the problem (**a common task), ask..
Can you tell me a bit more about the problem?
How long have you been vomiting?
How long have you had diabetes?

How often do you get the abdominal pains?

How long do the spasms last?

What is the cough like?

What does the pain feel like?

Do you have any pain at the moment?

When did you have the accident?

When did you notice the rash?

Explaining a process or procedure is another common task – use step by step explanations and make sure you clarify understanding. You can also repeat the information in a **summary** to ensure that the patient understands clearly.

Reassuring a patient: there are several role plays where the patient (or parent) is anxious about something. Think of these situations:

anxious about an operation

child with burns – anxious about scarring

waiting for biopsy result after a breast biopsy – anxious about cancer diagnosis

grandparent with child who has epilepsy – anxious about risk of fitting

post heart attack – anxious about resuming normal activity including sexual activity

Let's look at a role play in the OET Speaking for Nurses section. As you can see, there are numerous communication strategies which you can showcase. Remember that you are showing **how well you communicate.** There are very few medical terms in the role play (scarring, dermatologist, second degree burns). Most of the role play centres around the conversation that you (the nurse) have with the patient's mother.

Look at the examples of the language functions you might use during the role play.

1. Introducing yourself and starting the conversation

2. Calming a patient

3. Asking to repeat information

4. Asking to slow down

5. Clarifying information

6. Asking open questions

7. Using non-verbal communication

8. Reassuring (empathise then reassure)

9. Explaining a process

10. Bringing person back onto the topic

11. Explaining possible outcomes

12. Rounding up and close a conversation

12.OET READING STRATEGIES
Efficient reading skills

Skimming to get an overall impression.

Skimming is useful when you want to survey a text to get a general idea of what it is about. In skimming you ignore the details and look for the main ideas. **Main ideas are usually found in the first sentences of each paragraph and in the first and last paragraphs.** It is also useful to pay attention to the organisation of the text.

As reading is an interactive process, you have to work at constructing the meaning of the text from the marks on the paper. You need to be active all the time when you are reading. It is useful, therefore, if you need to read the text in detail, before you start reading to activate the knowledge you have about the topic of the text and to formulate questions based on this information. Skimming a text for gist can help you formulate questions to keep you interacting with the text.

Skimming a text using first lines of paragraphs.

In most academic writing, the paragraph is a coherent unit, about one topic, connected to the previous and next paragraphs.

Paragraphs are organised internally and the first sentence of each paragraph is often a summary of, or an introduction to, the paragraph. You can therefore get a good idea of the overall content of a text by reading the first sentence of each paragraph. This should help you get a feeling for the structure of the text. In many cases that will be enough, but if it isn't, you will now have a good idea of the structure of the text and you will find it easier to read in detail. Familiar texts are easier to read.

As reading is an interactive process, you have to work at constructing the meaning of the text from the marks on the paper. You need to be active all the time when you are reading. It is useful, therefore, if you need to read the text in detail, before you start reading to activate the knowledge you have about the topic of the text and to formulate questions based on this information. Skimming a text using first lines of paragraphs can help you formulate questions to keep you interacting with the text

The reading test is common to all candidates.

Part A – gap fill

This section will present you will four texts on the same topic. The texts will give you four different perspectives of the topic. Sometimes same or similar information may appear in more than one text, however, it may just be a 'missing piece'. For example, Text A may give you figures for 2007 and 2011 while a table in Text C may give you figures for 1979, 1986, 1995 and 2008.

There are several types of texts which you might find in Part A.

1. **An academic report on a study** – this will be set out in a particular way with sections like Background, Authors, Objectives, Results and so on.

2. **An article** which might be found in a professional journal or on a website. For example, an information piece about the risk of cannabis use.

3. **A personal story** – explaining a person's experience with the condition or disease. This may be written as the person speaks so it may be a bit less formal. It may also be a **case study** – a brief description of the experience.

4. **Statistics.** Notice the headings of the columns. If years are in the headings e.g. 1973, 1983, you may be asked to comment on the changes in something over the given years. Has it gone up or down, for example? Perhaps you have to compare countries or male and female.

The table should have a heading which tells you the general topic idea.

Let's look at the sample reading test from the OET website. The texts are about vasectomy. It's a good idea to print out all the information for this test before we go on.

You will have to complete around 29 gap fills for this part of the test. Notice that the gap fill text in the answer booklet has four paragraphs. This means that all the questions are found in one text - usually all but beware – sometimes you need to look in another paragraph for one answer.

The skills that you are being asked to use in the reading test are these ones:

1. Skimming for information. This means being able to skim over the text as a whole to pick out the general theme of the text. The first task when skimming is to look at the heading.

Ask yourself: 'What is the heading of the text telling me?'

Look at Text A1. The heading is called the **title** because this text is an academic report.

Title: Risk of Prostate Cancer after Vasectomy (2003)

The keywords are :   risk...prostate cancer....vasectomy

And possibly the date – 2003

Now you have the idea of what might be in text A1. You do not read any more.

You move onto Text A2. This is an example of a statistics text. There are 2 boxes in this text. Look at the general heading - **Vasectomy Studies from Britain (2008).** This tells you what the topic is. Then you need to see what the difference is between the 2 boxes. Looking at the headings of the boxes you can see that Box 1 is about **men 16-69, 2001 – 2008 (**so this one looks at changes in the numbers of a large group over the years.

Box 2: percentage of year groups..in 2008

Text A3: The heading is clear – **a FAQ leaflet on vasectomy**

Text A4: This is a case study about **vasectomy reversal.**

As you skim you should pick up the name **Gary** and you may also pick up his wife's name, **Sarah.**

I've just talked about the first thing to do when you skim, that is to look at the heading. The next area to skim is the first sentence. This is often called the **topic sentence.** This is because it gives you the **topic.**

Text A 1 doesn't have a topic sentence because it is presented as a report. Text A2 also does not have a topic sentence because it is a statistics table.

Text A3 – This text has 3 topics i.e. 3 questions e.g. **Q: How will I feel after the operation?**

Text A4: This text is an example of a text which you may need to read a few lines of to understand what it is about and before you reach the key words i.e vasectomy...reverse vasectomy.

2. Scanning

Now you are going to scan the texts to pick out **only the information you need to answer the question.** This is why you are advised NOT TO READ the whole text. You don't have time to do this and it is not necessary.

Work out which text relates to each paragraph. Looking at the paragraph with questions 1-3 you should notice the phrase <u>Statistics for 2008</u>. Where have you seen that before? That's from Text 2.

Now, move onto the next paragraph in the gap fill. Skim the paragraph to try and pick up key words. The first is 'serious risks or complications'. You can also see these terms in Text A3.

The third paragraph mentions some numbers. 40 and 75. It also mentions 'control group' so you know it is about a study. That's A1.

The last paragraph includes the key term **'reversal'.** This must be Text 4. But, notice that at the end of the paragraph (question 27) there is mention of **'Statistics from Britain for 2008'.** That means you are back to looking at A2 again.

Filling in the gap fill questions:

(1) This asks you about a statistic and the gap fill is _____ **of.** This means you need a percentage number. If it is a numeral in the text – write a numeral. For example, the answer is 18%.

(2) The next gap is 'under _____ in Britain' so you know you need a number not a percentage. Write a number If the text has a number – the answer here is 70. If the text has the number as a word e.g. 'ten', then you write the word not the number - 'ten' not '10'.

(3) This question asks you to comment on **changes in the statistics.** You are going to comment about whether the percentages went down, went up or stayed the same. Look at the answers and notice that you can use a variety of expressions to mean 'the numbers more or less stayed the same'.

Look at the table below with some expressions you can use to describe changes.

Goes down	Stays the same or almost the same	Goes Up
lowering (adj)	remain the same	increase in
go down	remain stable	surge in
plummet	are static	go up
a decline in	has not deviated from the norm	increasing (adj)
to lower	is steady	a rise in
a reduction in	is constant	escalate
a decrease in	is almost unchanged	
drop in	the results are consistent	
The numbers have eased.	is roughly the same	
	the results are similar	

Text 3: Questions 4 - 12

(4) This question gets you to change 'there are no known serious long-term health risks …by having a vasectomy' to

Vasectomy is a procedure without serious risks'.

Notice that there are several options which mean the same:

There are no known risks.

without any known risks.

with no known risks.

free of any known risks.

(5) Look for the key term *local anaesthetic* and you find the sentence part:

The large majority of men having a vasectomy will have a local anaesthetic..

This is asking you to paraphrase 'the large majority'. Notice that there are several options.

The large majority of men have the vasectomy under local anaesthetic.

The operation, which is **normally** carried out under local anaesthetic....

The operation, which is **generally** carried out under local anaesthetic....

The operation, which is **usually** carried out under local anaesthetic....

The operation, which is **in most cases** carried out under local anaesthetic....

The operation, which is **most often** carried out under local anaesthetic....

(6) This gap fill is a little difficult as the key words you are looking for are *pain, bruising* and *swelling* or similar words. The difficulty is that 'pain' is mentioned several times. In this case you are looking for a reference to all three terms. This is in the first sentence:

(Text) Your scrotum will probably be bruised, swollen and painful.

(Answer) – experience pain from bruising and swelling of his **scrotum.**

(7) This is an easy one – find the key terms *wear* and *support.* ....

General advice is to wear **tight-fitting underpants (or underwear)**

(8) This is an example of converting one grammatical form into another:

      active form → passive form

      verb → noun

      noun → verb

      adjective → adverb

The text says '**You should avoid strenuous exercise'** (active) which becomes

      Physical exertion should be avoided (passive)

(9) Similar to (8) -   first, look for 'infection' and you find:

Occasionally, some men **have** bleeding, a large swelling, or **an infection.**

If the site becomes **infected ...**

(10) You need to look for *months ..form....leakage of sperm.*

   In this case, **collect as sperm granulomas** is the same as **(sperm) granulomas** may form.

(11) This is a change from a verb into a noun phrase:

(Text) ...sperm may **leak** ....in the **surrounding tissue.**

(Answer) if there is any **leakage** of sperm into the <u>**surrounding tissue.**</u>

(12) This is a change from (Text) **...they can be treated** to

(Answers) **these can be painful but are** <u>**treatable.**</u>

Answers 13 – 20   Text 1

(13) This is a use of a similar expression:

Men with vasectomies do not have a higher risk of prostate cancer.

Men with vasectomies have been shown not to have a higher risk of prostate cancer.

Men with vasectomies **are not** at a higher risk of prostate cancer.

Men with vasectomies **have been shown not to be** at a higher risk of prostate cancer.

(14) Look for the key terms *40 and 75*. Notice the text says 'between 40 and 75' so that's OK. This is a simple case of looking for a number – **923**

(15) diagnosed with _____ means you are looking for a disease or a condition.

  prostate cancer.

(16) In the preceding _____ months – means you are looking for a number or the word 'few'.   **3 to 15.** Note that there is also a change from the noun 'diagnosis' in the text with the verb 'diagnosed with' in the answer.

(17) This is a more difficult question – find the term *'matching'* and reference to *control group.*

Controls.................with frequency **matching** to cases in 5-year age groups.

(Answer)   A control group of men with a matching <u>**age**</u> profile...

(18) This also a more difficult question – you find *relative risk* and look for a reference to length of time. – (Text) Relative risk (RR) ....nor with time since vasectomy.

Answer – The length of time since **vasectomy / a vasectomy / surgery.**

(19) and (20) are easy answers – matter of finding the key terms *'social class' 'of prostate cancer'*. The missing terms are easy to find – **family history...religious affiliation**

Text 4 - questions 21 – 26

(21) This appears to be an easy question but it is a little difficult. Your first thought may be that 'vasectomy is not intended to be a permanent change'. The answer is '**a** <u>temporary</u> **change'.**

(22)   This is another relatively easy question – the answer is **expensive.** It's a comprehension question where you need to work out that having two reversal operations might be expensive.

(23) This answer ' **two operations'** relates to the previous question.

(24) Easy question, obviously a number <u>**three children.**</u>

(25) The text says 'men under 40 should not rush into having one' – the answer is **(twenties and)** <u>**thirties.**</u>

(26) This is another example of a question with several options:

(Text)   There is the slightest chance that

(Answer)

They won't / don't ever want

They won't want any

They would never want

They do not want

Questions 27 – 29 - Text 2

(27) Answer with several options:

(Text) You have to comprehend the statistics for this one.

Statistics ....seem to <u>**support**</u> this advice.

Statistics ....seem to <u>**confirm**</u> this advice.

Statistics ....seem to <u>**verify**</u> this advice.

Statistics ....seem to <u>**reflect**</u> this advice.

Statistics ....seem to <u>**corroborate**</u> this advice.

Statistics ....seem to <u>**correspond with**</u> this advice.

(28) and (29) Both question asks about percentages –from Box 2. - 1% and 30%

13. Prepare yourself for the OET Listening test

The OET Listening test is one test for all Healthcare Professionals. This means that you may be presented with a listening text which has specific vocab from a profession other than your own. This can be a challenge as the OET covers a wide range of health professionals.

There are 2 sections to the listening test: one section (part A) is usually a dialogue and the other section (part B) is usually in the form of a mini talk or a lecture type of listening.

Remember that even though you hear the listening test once only, it is not all at once. You will listen to short sections then there will be a pause for you to write your answers. If you are unsure of an answer and the speaker starts the next section – forget about the answer you are unsure of. Concentrate on listening to the next section. Some questions ask you to write several words in the answer – write as many as you can in the time and prepare to listen to the next section.

Look at the guidance on the official OET website to give you an idea of what you can expect to find in parts A and B. Notice that you are advised to predict what you may be about to hear. Use any headings which signpost the sort of language you may hear.

If the listening text speaks about a study or research, you will expect to hear numbers and percentages. You may also hear words like *increased, decreased, deficit in, oversupply of* etc. Start a list of words which describe these changes so you are familiar with them.

When you take notes, don't write a whole sentence – there is no time for this. Start a glossary of abbreviations and get used to writing them. For example, an arrow pointing up ↑ can be used to mean *increase in, over*. Use abbreviations for common words e.g. *imp.* rather than writing *important*.

Good listening skills require you to be able to pick out key words. Your brain will start to fill in the extra words used in the sentence. The speaker may emphasise key words a little but in any case, you will mostly hear two or three key words in each sentence. When I talk about *key words* I mean the terms that are essential to the sentence. The sentence could almost have meaning just with these key words.

Here is an example from an ABC Health Report titled 'A study compared paracetamol with ibuprofen for fever in young children.'

"Ibuprofen and paracetamol, **fever reducers**, probably should be reserved for **children** with a temperature of **over 38.5°** celcius (sic) ; and who have **aches and pains** as well."

The key words here are : **fever reducers, children , over 38.5°, aches and pains**

So, how can you practise listening for key words? The OET website suggests listening to podcasts from ABC Radio National Health Report and BBC Health. Both sites have very good podcasts on a range of health topics , however, the benefit of the ABC Health Report is that you can also read the transcript of the talk. Try to listen once without looking at the transcript. Make notes only using abbreviations and key words. Then listen again while reading the transcript. How did you go? If possible, print out the transcript and highlight the key terms. Listen again and notice if the speaker puts any emphasis on the key terms or pauses after the key terms.

Another important thing is to revise medical terminology. Make sure you know as many medical prefixes and suffixes and the terms used in anatomy and physiology. Some people find it easy to read medical terminology because it is similar to their own language. However, the terms may be pronounced differently so listening is more difficult.

Find topics in all of the OET subgroups and try to identify any vocabulary which may crop up frequently. For instance, physiotherapy topics may use vocabulary which includes terms of movement, exercise and mobility. Podiatry topics may centre around the foot and toenails.

It is obvious that you will find it easier to listen to a topic which is even slightly familiar. Even if you have seen and heard some of the vocabulary, the listening will be easier. When you learn the medical terms, make sure you learn the pronunciation as well. Sites like thefreedictionary and Merriam Medical dictionary have a pronunciation button which lets you hear the term as well as read it. This also helps you to write the terms quickly without worrying about spelling.

Finally, think about the structure of the listening text. If it is a dialogue it will follow the structure of a conversation. I mean that there will be the introduction to the problem or issue then an explanation and perhaps some clarification of what was said. Finally, the conversation will round up and close.

If the listening text is a lecture, there will be an introduction to the lecture, a discussion of a few points then a conclusion. In a 5 minute talk you will expect to hear 3 to 4 points. There may also be lists e.g. of symptoms or side effects of medication. The test booklet will guide you as to the number you are expecting to hear.

The best way to practise listening is to listen to as much as you can and as often as you can. If you are not studying OET in an English-speaking country, then make use of the podcasts I have mentioned as well as listening to as many English language texts as possible.

Don't forget to practise basic listening skills. For example,

1. Listen for emphasis (more stress) on important words.

2. Listen for changes in intonation. (voice going up or down).

3. Listen for the key words in each sentence. Usually 1-2 main words. Listen for nouns and

'defining terms' e.g. words like *never, usually, mostly, always.*

4. Listen to the tone of voice - is the person angry, sad, tired.

http://www.examenglish.com/FCE/fce_listening_part1.htm
short conversation audio clips   - answer 1 multi choice question

http://englishteststore.net/index.php?option=com_content&view=article&id=225&Itemid=273
English lectures
conversations
gap fills

http://esltutorblog.com/listening.html

Lightning Source UK Ltd.
Milton Keynes UK
UKOW05f1831120118
316012UK00006B/117/P